Full **STEAM** Ahead!

Science Starters

From Seed to Pumpkin

Crystal Sikkens

CRABTREE
PUBLISHING COMPANY
WWW.CRABTREEBOOKS.COM

Title-Specific Learning Objectives:

Readers will:

- Explain that a life cycle is a series of changes that happens to a living thing in its lifetime.
- Describe the life cycle of a pumpkin using learned vocabulary.
- Use images to identify key ideas and features at each stage of a pumpkin's life cycle.

High-frequency words (grade one)	Academic vocabulary
a, are, did, has, have, in, is, it, the, you	female, life cycle, male, roots, seeds, sprout, stem, vine

Before, During, and After Reading Prompts:

Activate Prior Knowledge and Make Predictions:

Have children read the title and look at the cover images. Ask children:

- Have you picked a pumpkin before? When?
- Do you think the pumpkin in the picture on the cover is done growing? What about the pumpkin on the title page? Can you tell the title page is showing a pumpkin?

During Reading:

After reading page 10, examine the diagram. Ask:

- Do you notice the words on the diagram? What are they? (The words are labels.)

Explain that labels help us to identify the parts of something, and how they fit or work together.

- How do the labels help us understand what a pumpkin looks like at this stage? (They help us notice changes in appearance, such as the seed.)
- What else does the diagram help us understand? (How roots look—we don't usually see them.)

After Reading:

Together with children, make a list of key words that describe each step of the life cycle.

Have children work in groups to arrange the words in the correct order and draw pictures to illustrate.

To my sweet little pumpkin Jessica Ann Sikkens, with all my love

Author: Crystal Sikkens
Series Development: Reagan Miller
Editor: Janine Deschenes
Proofreader: Melissa Boyce
STEAM Notes for Educators: Janine Deschenes
Guided Reading Leveling: Publishing Solutions Group
Cover, Interior Design, and Prepress: Samara Parent
Photo research: Crystal Sikkens

Production coordinator: Katherine Berti
Photographs:
Dreamstime: Dleonis: p. 12
Dwight Kuhn: p. 6, p. 20
Getty images: Andre Lima: p. 15
iStock: redmal: p. 9; paladin13: p. 11; 2Ban: p. 18 (left);
    Panama7: p. 18 (right)
All other photographs by Shutterstock

Library and Archives Canada Cataloguing in Publication

Sikkens, Crystal, author
        From seed to pumpkin / Crystal Sikkens.

(Full STEAM ahead!)
Includes index.
Issued in print and electronic formats.
ISBN 978-0-7787-6189-1 (hardcover).--
ISBN 978-0-7787-6236-2 (softcover).--ISBN 978-1-4271-2255-1 (HTML)

        1. Pumpkin--Life cycles--Juvenile literature. 2. Pumpkin--Seeds--
Juvenile literature. I. Title.

SB347.S55 2019   j635'.62   C2018-906155-3
                                                            C2018-906156-1

Library of Congress Cataloging-in-Publication Data

Names: Sikkens, Crystal, author.
Title: From seed to pumpkin / Crystal Sikkens.
Description: New York, New York : Crabtree Publishing Company,
    [2019] | Series: Full STEAM ahead! | Includes bibliographical
    references and index.
Identifiers: LCCN 2018056582 (print) | LCCN 2018059398 (ebook) |
    ISBN 9781427122551 (Electronic) |
    ISBN 9780778761891 (hardcover : alk. paper) |
    ISBN 9780778762362 (pbk. : alk. paper)
Subjects: LCSH: Pumpkin--Seeds--Juvenile literature. | Pumpkin--
    Growth--Juvenile literature.
Classification: LCC SB347 (ebook) | LCC SB347 .S57 2019 (print) |
    DDC 635/.62--dc23
LC record available at https://lccn.loc.gov/2018056582

Printed in the U.S.A./042019/CG20190215

Table of Contents

Crabtree Publishing Company

www.crabtreebooks.com   1-800-387-7650

Published in Canada
Crabtree Publishing
616 Welland Ave.
St. Catharines, Ontario
L2M 5V6

Published in the United States
Crabtree Publishing
PMB 59051
350 Fifth Avenue, 59th Floor
New York, New York 10118

Published in the United Kingdom
Crabtree Publishing
Maritime House
Basin Road North, Hove
BN41 1WR

Published in Australia
Crabtree Publishing
Unit 3 – 5 Currumbin Court
Capalaba
QLD 4157

What is a Pumpkin?

Did you know a pumpkin is a fruit? A fruit is a part of a plant. Plants are living things.

seeds

Fruits have **seeds** inside them. Each time a seed is planted, it begins a new life cycle. A life cycle is the changes that happen to a living thing during its life.

What do Pumpkins Need?

sunlight

air

water

soil

A pumpkin plant needs soil, water, air, and sunlight to live and grow. Without these, it cannot finish its life cycle.

Air is all around. We cannot see it.

Most pumpkins begin their life cycle in late May or June. They finish their life cycle in September or October.

People pick pumpkins when they are fully grown.
To pick something is to take it from where it grew.
Have you ever picked a pumpkin?

Start with a Seed

A pumpkin begins its life cycle as a seed. First, the seed is placed in the ground and covered with soil.

seed

Pumpkin seeds are planted in rows or on small hills.

Soon, the pumpkin seed opens.
Roots grow down into the soil.

roots

Roots take in water from the soil. The water helps the pumpkin grow.

Soon, There's a Sprout

Next, a **sprout** grows above the ground. A sprout has a **stem** and two **leaves**.

The first leaves on the sprout are called seed leaves.

seed leaves

stem

seed

roots

The seed leaves take in sunlight and air. They use the sunlight and air to make food with water from the roots.

Pumpkin sprouts grow best where there is a lot of sunlight.

New Leaves

Soon, the sprout grows new leaves. These leaves are called true leaves.

true leaves

seed leaves

The true leaves now make the food for the plant.

After the plant grows many true leaves, the seed leaves fall off.

Very Long Vines

Next, a long **vine** begins to grow.
More vines will soon grow off the first vine.

vine

Stems and leaves grow on the vines. They help make food for the plant.

Small roots grow under each stem on the vines. The roots take in water to help make food. They also help hold the vines to the ground.

pumpkin

root

Flower Powder

Some stems on the vines grow flowers. The vines grow male and female flowers.

Bees carry yellow powder called **pollen** from the male flower to the female flower.

A female flower has a small ball below it. The ball will grow into a pumpkin.

female flower

pumpkin

First, the female flower needs pollen from the male flower.
Then, the ball begins to grow into a pumpkin.

Changing Pumpkins

Most young pumpkins are green.
They change color as they grow.
Many green pumpkins turn orange.

Most young pumpkins are green. This young pumpkin is starting to turn orange.

Some fully grown pumpkins are green and orange. Others are blue, white, or other colors!

Fully grown pumpkins are picked from the vine. A pumpkin's insides are used for food, such as pumpkin pie.

People cook and eat pumpkin seeds too.

New Life

Some pumpkins are not picked. They rot, or break down. Seeds from these pumpkins can grow into new pumpkin plants.

People can keep seeds from picked pumpkins. They plant them in the spring. Then, the life cycle repeats.

Words to Know

leaves [leevz] noun
Parts of a plant attached
to a stem that take in
sunlight and air

pollen [POL-uh-n] noun
Yellow powder or dust
found inside flowers

root [root] noun A part
of a plant that grows
underground and takes
in water

seed [seed] noun A part
of a plant that grows into
a new plant

sprout [sprout] noun
New growth from a seed;
also called a seedling

stem [stem] noun A part
of a plant that supports
leaves, flowers, or fruit

vine [vahyn] noun A
long, thin plant part that
grows along the ground
or around a support

A noun is a person, place, or thing.

A verb is an action word that tells you what someone or something does.

An adjective is a word that tells you what something is like.

Index

About the Author

Crystal Sikkens has been writing, editing, and providing photo research for Crabtree Publishing since 2001. She has helped produce hundreds of titles in various subjects. She most recently wrote two books for the popular Be An Engineer series.

To explore and learn more, enter the code at the Crabtree Plus website below.

www.crabtreeplus.com/fullsteamahead

Your code is:
fsa20

STEAM Notes for Educators

Full STEAM Ahead is a literacy series that helps readers build vocabulary, fluency, and comprehension while learning about big ideas in STEAM subjects. *From Seed to Pumpkin* includes labeled images and sequence words to help readers describe key details about a pumpkin's life cycle. The STEAM activity below helps readers extend the ideas in the book to build their skills in arts, science, and engineering.

Building a Life Cycle Model

Children will be able to:
- Describe and display the steps in a pumpkin's life cycle, and the features at each step.
- Create a 3-D model that represents a pumpkin's life cycle.

Materials
- Model Planning Sheet
- Tools for model, such as glue, tape, clay or plasticine, pipe cleaners, craft sticks, large and small pieces of cardboard, construction paper, crayons, paint, rocks, beads, etc.

Guiding Prompts
After reading *From Seed to Pumpkin*, ask:
- What is a life cycle? Can you name the steps of a pumpkin's life cycle?
- How does a pumpkin's life cycle repeat?

Activity Prompts
Explain to children that they will create a 3-D model that represents a pumpkin's life cycle. Review concepts with children:
- A model is a representation of a real thing.
- Engineers and scientists often use models to show how something works.
- 3-D means "three dimensional." A 3-D object has length, width, and depth. Show children 3-D and 2-D objects to illustrate.

Children will work in small groups to create their models on large pieces of cardboard. Hand each child a Model Planning Sheet. Review the stages and write them on a class anchor chart:
1. A seed is planted and roots grow.
2. A sprout grows above the ground. Seed leaves grow on the sprout.
3. The sprout grows true leaves. The seed leaves fall off.
4. A long vine grows. There are true leaves and small roots on the vine.
5. A flower grows on the vine. A small ball behind the flower is a baby pumpkin.
6. The young, green pumpkin grows on the vine.
7. The pumpkin is now orange and fully grown.

Hold a gallery walk for children to view their peers' models. Have them write comments on sticky notes to leave on models.

Extensions
- Children can make a technology connection by using digital cameras to take pictures of each stage of their models, and create a slide show that shows the stages of the life cycle.

To view and download the worksheet, visit **www.crabtreebooks.com/resources/printables** or **www.crabtreeplus.com/fullsteamahead** and enter the code **fsa20**.